IN
WIND'S
EDGE

OTHER BOOKS BY RALPH J. MILLS, JR.

POETRY

Door to the Sun (1974)
A Man to his Shadow (1975)
Night Road/Poems (1978)
Living with Distance (1979)
With No Answer (1980)
March Light (1983)
For a Day (1985)
Each Branch: Poems 1976–1985 (1986)
a while (1989)
Nine Poems (1993)
A Window in Air (1993)

CRITICISM

Theodore Roethke (1963)
Contemporary American Poetry (1965)
Richard Eberhart (1966)
Edith Sitwell (1966)
Kathleen Raine (1967)
Creation's Very Self (1969)
*Cry of the Human: Essays on
    Contemporary American Poetry* (1975)

BOOKS EDITED

*On the Poet and his Craft: Selected Prose
    of Theodore Roethke* (1965)
Selected Letters of Theodore Roethke (1968)
The Notebooks of David Ignatow (1973)
Open Between Us [Essays and Interviews of
    David Ignatow] (1980)

IN
WIND'S
EDGE

POEMS BY
RALPH J.
MILLS, JR.

ASPHODEL PRESS

MOYER BELL

Wakefield, Rhode Island & London

Published by Asphodel Press

First Edition

Library of Congress Cataloging-in-Publication Data

Mills, Ralph J.
    In wind's edge : poems / by Ralph J. Mills, Jr. — 1st ed.
        p.   cm.
    ISBN 1-55921-187-3 (alk. paper)
    I. Title.
PS3563.I4233I5   1997
811'.54—20   96-44932
                                                      CIP

Cover design: Natalie Mills Bontumasi

Printed in the United States of America.
Distributed by Publishers Group West,
Box 8843, Emeryville, CA 94662, 1-800-788-3123
(in California 1-510-658-3453)

In memory of my mother & father
and
for Helen, Natalie, David, & Lucian,
Julian, & Brett

What changes.
Is the weather
all there is.
—Robert Creeley

locale is
the sky partly
—Larry Eigner

CONTENTS

ACKNOWLEDGMENTS

Thanks are due the editors of the following periodicals and anthology in which many of these poems appear, occasionally in different versions:

> *The American Poetry Review, Another Chicago Magazine, Chicago Review, Eureka Literary Magazine, The Illinois Review, Indelible Ink, Lift, LVNG, Mississippi Valley Review, Northeast, The North Stone Review, Object Permanence* (Glasgow), *Private Arts, Spoon River Quarterly, Tar River Poetry,* and *For David Ignatow: An Anthology,* edited by Robert Long (Guild Hall/Cassio's Editions, 1994). A group of these poems, some in differing versions, was published as *Nine Poems* (Tel Let 26, 1993). Thanks to John Martone.

Special thanks also to Michael Anania, Michael Barrett, Hayden Carruth, Jim Elledge, Theodore Enslin, Dale Heiniger, David Ignatow, Devin Johnston, Milton Kessler, James Laughlin, Peter Manson, Hilda Morley, John Frederick Nims, Robert Schuler, and Lucien Stryk for various kinds of encouragement and support.

R. J. M., Jr.

MARCH ONE'S

march one's
                    sun
high as these branches,
                        tight ice–
cover gone
            & dry wiry
vine, plant stubble
show brown or grey,
                    though a
close eye finds
                dots, threads,
flecks blushing
to tips
            —a way
        out a way in—
                            trees
bow, wind keeps
them in tow,
            limbs fling a slippery
net / it
lets go:
            one bar of sunlight
passes through glass,
                        this lacquered table
edge
steadily glowing—

THIRD OF/MARCH

third of
march—
          unleafed
vines loop,
tangle
on a ledge
          here &
     there
          a stretch of them reddened
startling as a blood
rush
     come among
this grey scrawl—

SKY/AT

sky
   at
light
   hazed blue
after rain—
     grass
        ap-
   pears
     / bare
weed, branch knuckle
thinly wet
     take
polish,
    each an issue
        of
        water
of still air—

FIRST/SOUND

first
        sound—
                bird's
whistle at
daybreak
        near where the
water is
        & trees
lean
    to get tested by
a wind that's
struck up
            —then sun
takes it,
        climbs the ridged
skin of locust,
            each fissure or
crack
spilling out light—

WHERE IS THIS

where is this
last of march
sky sliding

       grizzle
in it
      two
blue crocuses
      below a tree of
heaven
break cover
      rise
un-
opened
   /
      straight up &
high
   their held wings just
visible
     herring gulls
in a loose
group bugle
     bugle a-
  gain
    giving
notice—

WARM/UP

warm
up
     buttons knobs
along boughs
       get some
color
   even in
mist in soaked
air
   little
bits of translucency
        water
    globes the
under
side of high shoots
      & extending
their length
    for a
   breath or for sun
          three
     tulips all one
avid
red

SWAYED

swayed,
                those hang-
belly clouds —

    purple crab flowers, locust buds, cherry
limbs an
upshooting tangle
                    enmeshed over
          & between —
                    this
cold slips in
low,
      picked
off the shore waters —

NO/EDGE

            no
edge
            not a break
                        cloud to
cloud
            air's full of
grit, misting
with rain in occasional
spatters—

            yard tall, the
tulips
            pink
on pallor of green
stems
            stand
tranced
            unbent by
any lake wind
                        those petals en-
            folding
                        another sky's
light—

ANOTHER ONE

      thinking of
a river pigeons, gulls
pass across,
       grey-shadowed
on its green—
     afternoon light
drops between walls
       in rods, in rectangles
streaking the surface—
     *   *   *
      april cold's
here—
   a single window
frames the neighbors' trees,
       honey locust
rearing to
lash several maples just out of
reach—
     *   *   *
      a day
        another
one—
   further off
the river forks,
       channel east
to open
water
    & wind that's rising
        risen—

CLOUDED

clouded—
                    a sky's quick
turn
        in
        half light
                        scilla looking
blue as
still water
                        branches
lift rough
buds
        to rain
in the street
                    & forsythia's
tissue-thin yellow,
like stars,
                    when
wind enters
                    the shoots flex,
intent—

5/15

not yet
to full leaf,
         white cone
blossoms flaking,
            this
bird cherry
leaks
    a may
rain—

SHIMMER OF

        shimmer of
morning star
          clear
of the rain—
         beech, pin oak &
lilac sky
      : moon's
peel left there
          almost goes
missed—

A LITTLE/SUN

a little
      sun
touches this
locust,
      yellow birch
in curls—

        one mourning
dove flutes,
      repeats
out of back-
yard trees

        : the sky
changes—lunar
grey of dove's
      head,
feathers,
      its "diagnostic"
whistling wings—

IN LATE MAY

clouds
          the last gap of
blue closing—
               cold or
     not
               phlox
flowers out
               lavender whitened
below each petal's
edge
          which folds as
rain hits
               all the
trees just leafing
                    & breaks apart
the tulips
               their foot-high & more
stems left tipping
                         light-
headedly—

MAY COLUMBINE

—for David Ignatow

          may columbine
                         its
spurred
flowers gone—
               astilbe's
froth clusters,
            some nodding
      bells /
                  in one neighbor's tree
breeze stretches a
bough
         as to reach
out of
shade
         turn molten
green gold
            this long
moment the
sun's
sliding under—

A SLOW

a slow
kind of
breeze
    parting leaf
from leaf
     this deliberation
letting yarrow
soar
   formally
like flat-topped
milky clouds
       while the air
mists
silvered grey
    & a window blinks
distantly
     opalescent as though
some-
one you remember
remembered
     you
  there
    & who maybe
waved—

LU-/LUNA

lu-

      luna

black

    a half circle of

light

   then violet,

fog-grey /

    this time the

moon loses

itself

     someone calling

a name calls it

home—

     wind

      laying open the clouds

finds out these

      flower-

   heads,

       each

peony petal

    swift, a

winged thing—

THERE

there
heavy willow boughs
                        reach
to a pond's
calm shimmer,
                        dragging under
the end-leaves —

                        & there
over it a
pair of geese climb
                        honking
west where the sun
goes,
            necks at a stretch —

            there too
blue & violet
iris
            pressed together
match yellow-patched sepals
                        with slant light
            sinking
down past grass & the
fine grains —

BITS OF AIR

I

      into
   june
calm wind calm water
             nearly
no rain
      the tall
red & yellow
belled columbine
            petals
   astray
        aren't bothered by
what bits of air
shake these several
maples —

II

      humid blur, the high
layers
of dust
      a light
movement too
level with grass, cooling as you
reach down —
        who or what
is it travels across
          one body, one
leaf & spear to another
         touches them
at once —

A WIND/LAPS

a wind
laps at vines —
                green's
deepest where
leaves push close,
                cover each
other
with shadow
            & move
quicker than fish —

PURPLE/CRAB

      purple
crab, now the locust—

        uppermost leaves
on stick limbs writhe, churn
close to a foam
              in wind
currents
        —but
placid again
        as the sun lights up
blue through
every chicory petal
              this side
of the fence—

CLOSE, DAMP

 close, damp
bushes & porch
vines
 the heat in its
weight, a wavering
haze—
 now
 ripped cries, an
oversize crow beats a route
into
 & through
this maple's tall reaches,
 sets
 sparrows
 chittering,
then drags high
the sun—

CLOUDS ON THE

      clouds on the
    move
so little
"blue for you"
        the window
frames leaves,
      high
feathery
reach   :
    a locust tree
    four
floors up
     /   near-
      weightless petals of
impatiens
    white   coral   lavender
picked off in
    breezes
  twisting them round

HUMPS,/DIPS OF THIS

humps,
dips of this
empurpled
grey cloud
wind in the
trees changing leaf-
faces,
a
liquified
ripple, a swell—
& the park's
lake takes a turn,
willows
give in to it,
stiffen out
their spear-pointed
leaves,
close to dissolving
in air's
transparencies—

A/STREAKED

a
streaked sky
over
trees —
late
sun
on the branches,
wind slowed to
no motion
& these clusters
of tiny
white bells
stay
still
/
a
watcher
dissolves among
shadows patching
together
into one
lengthened-out
shape —

7/22

lit
now
     how the deep-
lobed maple
        fluttery locust
pull with a
wind
    stretching them
tight
in between

8/94

       northeast
blow
      :   shadow foliage flung
off green
        heaves, slithers,
climbs again
         in shaken
emanation
on the glass—

.

MAYBE

      cardinal a
rust
blur fast through the leaves,
                    sparrows
     there in congress
close by—
        maybe a walk
over fresh
park grass
      & maybe the bench
where i
felt sun once
         on its chipped &
cracked green,
           where the right afternoon
shade is
pitched from the trees—

SUCH/CLOUDING

            such
clouding
            the air shifts
thick through with damp—

            morning like twilight,
branches, leaves
                        lose
detail, fade
            shadow en-
circles them
                        while starlings
        seen
nowhere
keep mute—

YELLOW/FLASHES

       yellow
flashes—
              these daisies
black-eyed
susans
                centers, petals
from the sun—

                & what
clouds bulk
up
     at street's
end
        the september cold
ready to figure
itself in—

10/93

```
        what memory
of clouds
                the trees part-
way
unsleeved—
            a dry
            day, heat'll be
back up awhile
                    a
            while
                    these early
brief gusts
working higher—
                    third of
a moon straight
over me
            white as any
scratched stone
                    rim
powdering
            in dawn's
blue vapor—
```

ALL DAY

(Variation on Jaccottet)

all day these small voices the
birds not in sight
        hours
counted out among grass
blades on yellowed no
beaten-gold leaf
       sky this
fall
blue reaches wide & then wider

SKEINS,/TWISTS

—*for Michael Anania*

skeins,
      twists of
cottony cirrus,
      such textures
under so much
blue—

      trees lunge
from this wind,
      making
as though to
float down hill,
      leaves,
streamers drawn
behind,
      the bared branch
lengths clarified in
far air—

WIND/IN HERE

             wind
in here, a fine
chisel—
             now this down-
     curve,
                  afternoon
failing each day
                  —there's no
place to hold,
                  not an inch of
limb
        between one leaf's
yellow, the
next's
        unloosening
brown—

LATE DAYS

I

after a
      sixth day's
rain, the cover of
leaves mostly
down—
      a few blue
slits open
        between clouds
vanish fast   /
      the sky dense
again,
    cold here
for good—

II

    pigeons'
wings smack
      air   & lift
 —then two, no it's
three starlings
        tear among half-
leafless
vine berry clumps,
        red stems
flicked
by the wind—

III

        late days soon
begun : someone's small
yard willow
            sweeps
    an arc,
            rattling
frost-starched narrow leaves
                        pear
        yellow
raggedy green
            & this six o'clock
lopped moon
glows like ice—

EVENING SONG

late day flames
orange
        birds call
far off in dropping
wind
        on the lake
waves phosphoresce
                sun's
gone
the other way
                voices on a
bus or
up this street
                motes &
bits
        spun in cold air
falling where
feet scrape concrete
                names
thin syllables
break loose
                shadows fill
one shadow
beneath a tree
                overhead
clouds billow
                shred to
take new
shapes
        faces forms
dislocate
                yellowy
leaf dust
        circles
circling down

SKY/SWEPT

     sky
swept,
       whitened clouds glowing
gold-crisped at borders,
             higher
further
       blue pools
breaking them, ragged &
wide,
      the eye finds shape on
shape, reaches in deep,
            inventing
what's come
upon,
      whatever may be there

    —& here
         crush of brown
leaves under heel, ground
to powder,
      the dust in
coils, scattering,
         sent by rough
off-the-water
gusts—
      day's light
closes past
mid-november,
        windows,
streetlamps
blink on, those clouds, their
hollows dimmed now
           blue-grey
in retreat—

MELT-/DOWN

   melt-
down
    : wet
salt grime,
        a trickling
out
beneath drifts —
          & this
locust's
bony shape, wind
worrying it,
       tightened
vines smacking at
fence boards —
        now a west-
descending moon
          lowers its
humpbacked blue light,
           after five
nights' travel,
       wrapped
in cloud —

A BIRTHDAY

             a birthday—
& rain's into
snow
over broken pods,
                   splay
boughs wet
grey in grey light,
                   their shadowed
undersides
             driven up by
wind from which
flakes strike, sharply
whirled—

                   cold folds
the house walls, bushes,
trees,
        any
breath steams
here, clouds get lower—
                   near a window
i'm still—
             move
with no movement,
                   entering the
age of my father's
last year—

GREY/GREEN

grey

       green

ice on
the pond water—

         snow not
thick or
fast-falling

     sifts like a
persistent drizzle /
        willow
          wands toss
as the wind
begins

      : cherry, ash
tree
    pull back
& gather—

12/92

sun-
drenched, near
zero—

     shadows of cloud,
morning slips
across roof pitches
         with a life
the wind's own
       small trees
whir
     their wordless whipping
just here
      sharp-pointed
as sleet
      —it's bright, not
snowy
     the clock keeps
running on unseen
wheels, ratchets
       someone's breath
struggling
in tubes
     an invasion of
cells
     above her/him the
inextricable
tangled branches outside
panels of glass
      where a sky simply
bursts
blue, black or starlit
  & through—

        big cloud
                bundles
evenly stretched—

                  sleet
grates
without wind,
               falls a strict
vertical, birches
standing up
            rigid
into it,
          their bark, cracked
black,
         glows
moon-silver
               & day—
day's emptied west
—it's away

THE/GLOSS OF

                    the
gloss of
ice
     on a stiff-
jointed locust
                    rocking
side
wise—
          snow circles these
stone & brick
buildings
          which hover, wrinkle
like white fabric,
                    heavier
clouds leveling
down—
          dead pale stalks,
stumps
     & bushes that yank
at their roots
                    to an east wind's
prompting

MOON,/THE CLEAR STAR-

moon,
the clear star-
light
winds more than
edgy
engage these
pond willows
/ head to
head in night
dances,
low over ice a
click
clicking
of "sticks"

BLUE/SNOW

blue
snow
    in a line on
porch stairs—
        this blue too
defines cherry,
maple & seven foot haw,
      which don't
shift,
    air
withholding breath
at cloud-crowded
        day's
break,
    as snow
pales a
moment,
    then goes
grey, stains,
      so looking you
know
you're awake—

THE DWARF/MOON'S

the dwarf
moon's
        sunk
            sky
                an
uneven
striping of greys
                from which
                flakes
swirl a
        veil
                out of some
        wind current
                    or up-
            surge
                    slacking
into calm
            as
            snow goes
        on   layers
the ice plates
                in
narrows of north river
water—

CLOUDS/COME

clouds
come
to rain
placid
green wash of
river
twisted
in froth—
& the trees
begin
out front
of this house
crab, hawthorn
shudder with
wind—
a new year's
weak day-
light
settles on branches
& stays—

THEIR LINES/SKETCHED

  crow
cry
     caw caw-
ing out of
mist
        out of stripped
trees
        sparrows ride blowing
bushes, phone wires,
            keep a chatter
up   /
      morning
         whatever
       it is
           dissolves & dis-
colors in
sky above knotted limbs,
            wet
      crown twigs,
           their lines
sketched by eye on the air—

DEAD POET

(Variation on Supervielle)

    right

        now—hand

him an

ant, a spider

        anything

little to

hold

      beak of

    swallow

    sparrow

    wren

        put in his palm

slivers of rain-

damp grass

       changing

to green again

        let him

feel rough

red brick with each finger-

tip

     or pebbles

through his shoes—

         next to

nothing he's

been emptied out

under the moon,

      in this

void

laced with stars

        —but he'll

give back

song

     words dancing

sarabande as they call up what's

ungraspable as air,

        make hidden

light rise inside snow
                        or show
luminescent
domes of cloud piled at
the sky's far edge
                        —he sings name
on name,
            then offers
quiet too, its wide
erasure
            he who waits
alone & friendless,
                        steeped in the
shadow of a wall or spring-
flowering tree

FOG INLAND

fog inland : these
isolate thickets—
                    steady
drip off eaves,
            the black iron of
fire
ladders—
                    window's lifted
to rain, both hands
flat on its sill
                        there's wet
flashing where each
                        knotty ash, slick
length of maple
                    yields a
                little to wind
                            —breathe
in,   out
with them
                    & once
again in—

ONE LEVEL OF

one level of
snow
    thaws
along railings—
      berries here
shrunken to
knobs,
    grey
strung-out vines
caught in
      watery
ice—
    the back
yard:
    tall, aged
ailanthus
      splits its
big trunk in a
y,
    forking,
forks some more,
      black against
late winter
    sun's
surprise brightness—

    & south
gales cut loose
      suddenly
tumbling forsythia,
      a crow
squawks, half wheels
aloft—
    cardinals   sparrows—
      whee
    yaha
      wind's

in the branches /
　　　　　　　called from
sleep, pick up
this limb,
　　　　kick
heels, dance
　　　　for old
doc williams' sake—
　　　　　　　for march sprouts
& the trees ready to
break out—

TREES

(Variation on Jaccottet)

        up
out of this
ground,
        out of leaf
stems, bones, grains
          layer
    after layer
the wet dirt shines, the
rain—
      & trees take a hold
in sun's
slow addition :
          twigs,
    foliage
each day sifting
       more air—

ROUGH/THAW AIR

      rough
thaw air—
        limbs
in it
   bits
      weeds bowing
             the grasses
near flat—
          cloud wisps &
floaters
      rise
      fast
         south to
    southwest
         & a bird cherry
holds its moment
          silver as
birch
in the sun

WET HAZE

wet haze
            in its spread—
sun out through
branches—bulging knots
       gnarls
bud
nubs weakly green
              the birds
        among them
             vocal for rain
& bluff winds—

NO WIND HERE

no wind here
           to budge
a half-
leafed locust or
white birch
           whose shadows
lying out far
in the grass
           are dark
as root tunnels
under them—

SPLIT/TWIGS

split
twigs,
         some blossoms—
leaflets flip over,
                bird-jittery
green sieved with
gold light   /
               one wave
another
         these breezes, cloud
handfuls pushing for
change—

THEN LIFT

          then lift :
                    greening
branches rise
for light,
          a leaf
un-
peels
          then
     loosed clusters
                    /
                         like something
given
          one hand to the next
or
as this sun seen
                    feels
falling
into open palms—

HALF/CLOUDY

—for Lorine Niedecker

half
cloudy, mild—
      there's little so
good as dove
call
    or opening
of crocus /
      a window to
watch sun
on the shrubbery
          how thin &
uneven these
rows of trees,
        Lorine,
    but everything's
              coming
round
    again yellow,
fuzzed green—

SUN

sun
       & the wind's
strings
       : a few
    maples pulled
out of shadow
       shine
  wildly—

MOMENT

"is this the moment?"
—James Schuyler

patch of lily
tuft's raised
                & curls
green, shiny
                leaf shade
broadened
with sun
            the ferns
        un-
scrolling—
                a moment like
this
        when there'll
be no moments
                any
more—

CROCUS/FLICKER

crocus
      flicker—these
yellow or
blue
      flame shapes
in uncertain
light,
      a day's
cloudover—

        along the fence
forsythia,
        electric to the
air's
sure touch—

        with no
plans, aims
diminishing,
        step off
the porch
        into a sting
of april rain—

RED/TIPS

red
tips : tulips
up
un-
sheathing,

then hyacinths'
cool
white spikes
& scilla
in a tide the
sky-
blue
"of paradys"

WATCHING DAWN/TREES

      watching dawn
trees
          a spill-off
of rain
         on one leaf, the
other
       & straight
for the ground—

              the cup with its
stains, the table
& lamp,
        keys, shoes—
               this
day
     edging beyond
window glaze
         goes—

  a full blown honey locust
loose above
the neighboring roof—

IN WIND'S/EDGE

    in wind's
edge
     just now the
full scent of bird-
cherry
      blossoming
stirred—
       white
flowers,
       their cloud
come
down—

AN ASH/SWINGS

an ash
swings, see —
       grey
branchings hidden in
the full green
            wind drift's
got it, those
digit leaflets
        flick
with
underglimmer,
          wavery
ferns sink &
rise,
    above them wires over
roof slopes
       in silhouette
prop up sort of a
nimbus sky :
          the clouds alter
every
thing
    good bye now
  yes,
good bye

A Note

The poems "All day," "Night's come," "Where the ground" and "Trees" are based in varying degrees upon poems from *Airs* by Philippe Jaccottet (Paris: Gallimard, 1967). The poem "Dead poet" is similarly developed from a poem in Jules Supervielle: *Selected Writings* (New York: New Directions, 1967).